MW00893654

Print Handwriting
PRACTICE BOOK

 For Adults & Teens

THIS BOOK BELONGS TO

Improve your print writing skills with this book,
with letters tracing, words and motivational phrases,
The handwriting activity can be beneficial
by improving neural connections, cursive reading
ability, concentration and focus, fine motor skills.

2023 Bekalearn publishing

Print Handwriting Letters

A A A A A A A A A A A A A A A A
A A A A A A A A A A A A A A A A

a a a a a a a a a a a a a a a a a a
a a a a a a a a a a a a a a a a a a

B B B B B B B B B B B B B B B B
B B B B B B B B B B B B B B B B B

b b b b b b b b b b b b b b b b b b
b b b b b b b b b b b b b b b b b b

C C C C C C C C C C C C C C C C
C C C C C C C C C C C C C C C C C

c c c c c c c c c c c c c c c c c c
c c c c c c c c c c c c c c c c c c

A A A A A A A A A A A A A A
A A A A A A A A A A A A A A

a a a a a a a a a a a a a a a
a a a a a a a a a a a a a a a

B B B B B B B B B B B B B B
B B B B B B B B B B B B B B B

b b b b b b b b b b b b b b b
b b b b b b b b b b b b b b b

C C C C C C C C C C C C C
C C C C C C C C C C C C C C

c c c c c c c c c c c c c c c
c c c c c c c c c c c c c c c c

A A A A A A A A A A A A A A A A
A A A A A A A A A A A A A A A A

a a a a a a a a a a a a a a a a a
a a a a a a a a a a a a a a a a a

B B B B B B B B B B B B B B B B B
B B B B B B B B B B B B B B B B B

b b b b b b b b b b b b b b b b b
b b b b b b b b b b b b b b b b b

C C C C C C C C C C C C C C C
C C C C C C C C C C C C C C C C

c c c c c c c c c c c c c c c c c
c c c c c c c c c c c c c c c c c

A A A A A A A A A A A A A A A
A A A A A A A A A A A A A A A

a a a a a a a a a a a a a a a a a a a
a a a a a a a a a a a a a a a a a a a

B B B B B B B B B B B B B B B B
B B B B B B B B B B B B B B B B

b b b b b b b b b b b b b b b b b b b
b b b b b b b b b b b b b b b b b b

C C C C C C C C C C C C C C C
C C C C C C C C C C C C C C C C

c c c c c c c c c c c c c c c c c c c
c c c c c c c c c c c c c c c c c c c

D D D D D D D D D D D D D D D D D D D D

D D D D D D D D D D D D D D D D D D D

d d d d d d d d d d d d d d d d d d d d

d d d d d d d d d d d d d d d d d d d

E E E E E E E E E E E E E E E E E E E E

E E E E E E E E E E E E E E E E E E E

e e e e e e e e e e e e e e e e e e e e e

e e e e e e e e e e e e e e e e e e e

F F F F F F F F F F F F F F F F F F F F

F F F F F F F F F F F F F F F F F F F

f f f f f f f f f f f f f f f f f f f f f

f f f f f f f f f f f f f f f f f f f f

D D D D D D D D D D D D D D D D D D D D
D D D D D D D D D D D D D D D D D D D D

d d d d d d d d d d d d d d d d d d d d d
d d d d d d d d d d d d d d d d d d d d

E E E E E E E E E E E E E E E E E E E E E
E E E E E E E E E E E E E E E E E E E E E

e e e e e e e e e e e e e e e e e e e e e
e e e e e e e e e e e e e e e e e e e e e

F F F F F F F F F F F F F F F F F F F F F
F F F F F F F F F F F F F F F F F F F F F

f f f f f f f f f f f f f f f f f f f f f
f f f f f f f f f f f f f f f f f f f f f

D D D D D D D D D D D D D D D D D D D
D D D D D D D D D D D D D D D D D D D

d d d d d d d d d d d d d d d d d d d
d d d d d d d d d d d d d d d d d d

E E E E E E E E E E E E E E E E E E E E
E E E E E E E E E E E E E E E E E E E E

e e e e e e e e e e e e e e e e e e e e
e e e e e e e e e e e e e e e e e e e e

F F F F F F F F F F F F F F F F F F F F
F F F F F F F F F F F F F F F F F F F F

f f f f f f f f f f f f f f f f f f f f
f f f f f f f f f f f f f f f f f f f f

D D D D D D D D D D D D D D D D D D D D
D D D D D D D D D D D D D D D D D D D

d d d d d d d d d d d d d d d d d d d d
d d d d d d d d d d d d d d d d d d d

E E E E E E E E E E E E E E E E E E E E
E E E E E E E E E E E E E E E E E E E

e e e e e e e e e e e e e e e e e e e e e
e e e e e e e e e e e e e e e e e e e

F F F F F F F F F F F F F F F F F F F F
F F F F F F F F F F F F F F F F F F F F

f f f f f f f f f f f f f f f f f f f f f
f f f f f f f f f f f f f f f f f f f f

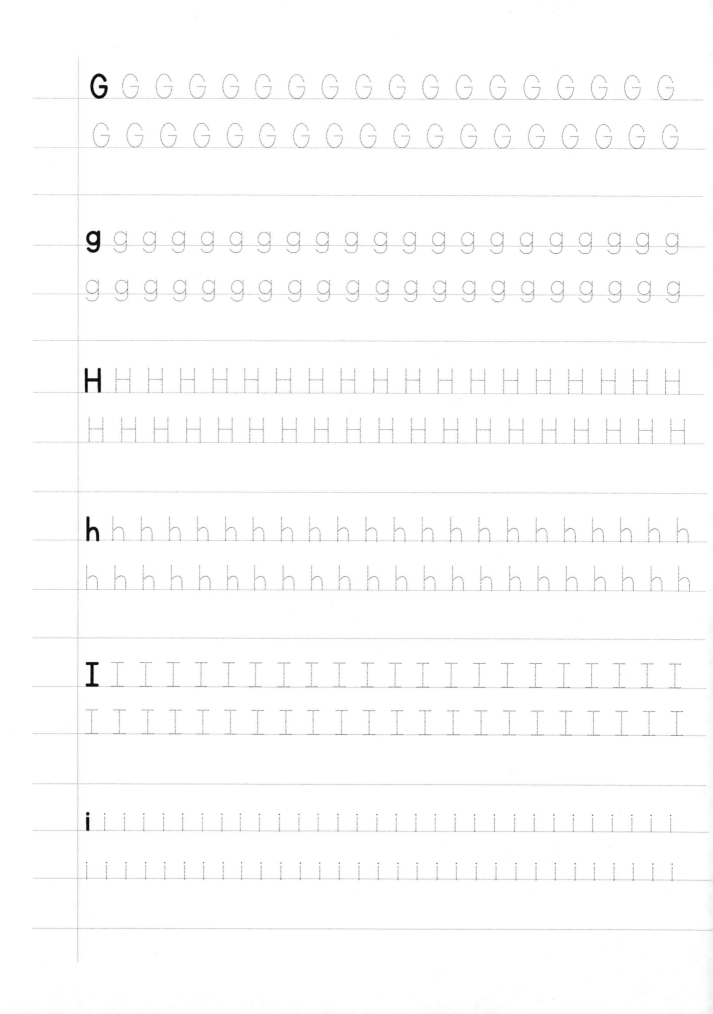

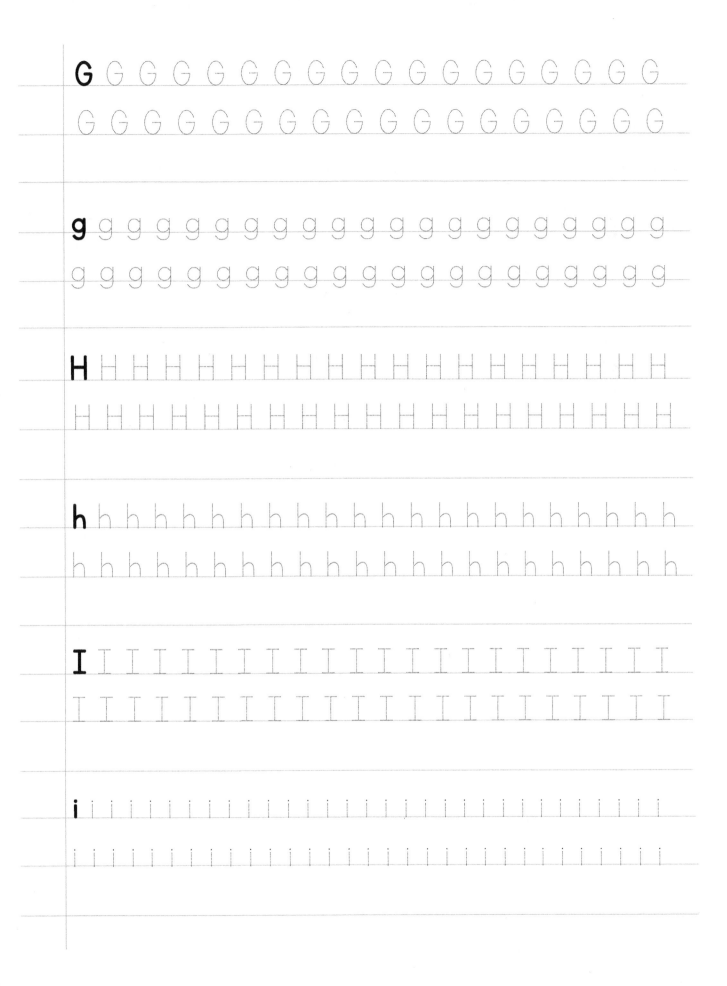

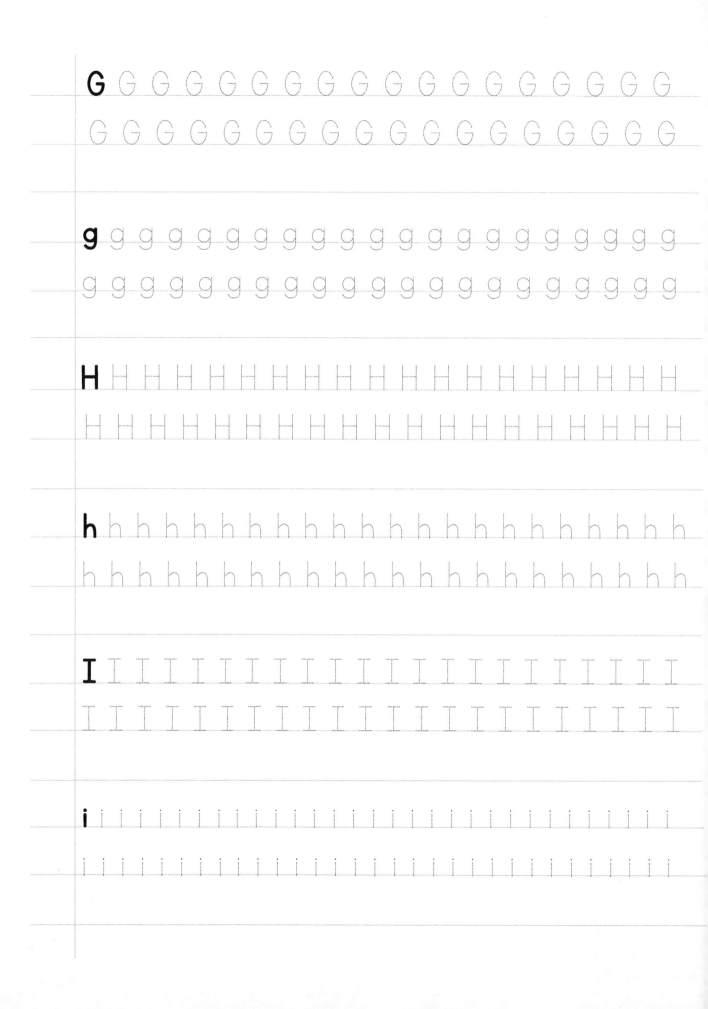

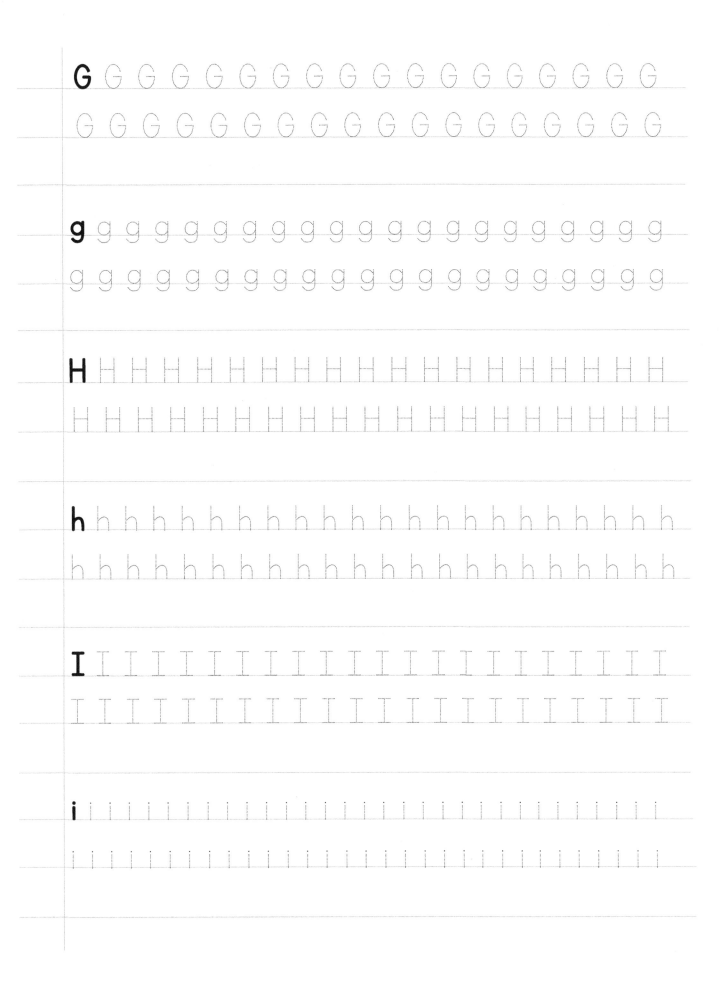

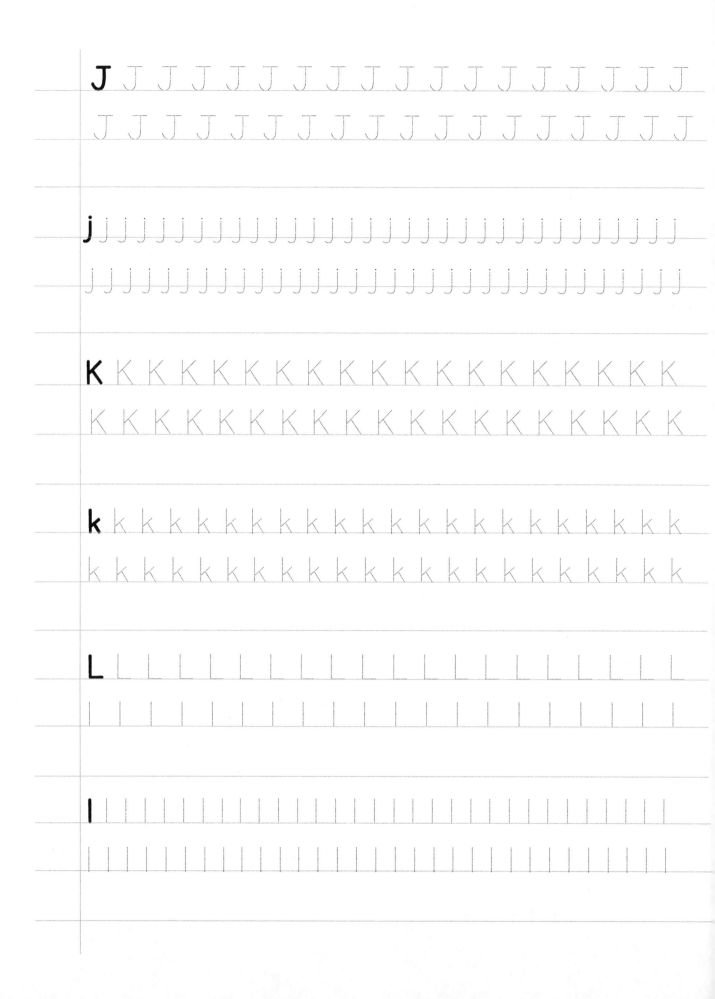

J J J J J J J J J J J J J J J J J J J J
J J J J J J J J J J J J J J J J J J J

j j j j j j j j j j j j j j j j j j j j j j j
j j j j j j j j j j j j j j j j j j j j j j

K K K K K K K K K K K K K K K K K K
K K K K K K K K K K K K K K K K K K K

k k k k k k k k k k k k k k k k k k k
k k k k k k k k k k k k k k k k k k k

L L L L L L L L L L L L L L L L L L L
l l l l l l l l l l l l l l l l l l l l l l l l

l l l l l l l l l l l l l l l l l l l l l l l l l l l l l l
l l l l l l l l l l l l l l l l l l l l l l l l l l l l l l

M MMMMMMMMMMMMMMMMMMM
MMMMMMMMMMMMMMMMMMM

m mmmmmmmmmmmmmmmmm
mmmmmmmmmmmmmmmmmm

N NNNNNNNNNNNNNNNNNN
NNNNNNNNNNNNNNNNNNN

n nnnnnnnnnnnnnnnnnnn
nnnnnnnnnnnnnnnnnn

O OOOOOOOOOOOOOOOOO
OOOOOOOOOOOOOOOOO

o ooooooooooooooooooooo
ooooooooooooooooooo

M M M M M M M M M M M M M M M
M M M M M M M M M M M M M M M

m m m m m m m m m m m m m m m
m m m m m m m m m m m m m m m

N N N N N N N N N N N N N N N
N N N N N N N N N N N N N N N N

n n n n n n n n n n n n n n n n
n n n n n n n n n n n n n n n

O O O O O O O O O O O O O O O
O O O O O O O O O O O O O O O

o o o o o o o o o o o o o o o o o o
o o o o o o o o o o o o o o o o

M M M M M M M M M M M M M M M M M M
M M M M M M M M M M M M M M M M M M

m m m m m m m m m m m m m m m m m
m m m m m m m m m m m m m m m m m

N N N N N N N N N N N N N N N N N N
N N N N N N N N N N N N N N N N N N

n n n n n n n n n n n n n n n n n n n
n n n n n n n n n n n n n n n n n n

O O O O O O O O O O O O O O O O O
O O O O O O O O O O O O O O O O O

o o o o o o o o o o o o o o o o o o o o o
o o o o o o o o o o o o o o o o o o o o

M M M M M M M M M M M M M M M M
M M M M M M M M M M M M M M M M

m m m m m m m m m m m m m m m
m m m m m m m m m m m m m m m m

N N N N N N N N N N N N N N N N
N N N N N N N N N N N N N N N N N

n n n n n n n n n n n n n n n n n
n n n n n n n n n n n n n n n n n

O O O O O O O O O O O O O O O O
O O O O O O O O O O O O O O O O

o o o o o o o o o o o o o o o o o o o
o o o o o o o o o o o o o o o o o

P PPPPPPPPPPPPPPPPPP
PPPPPPPPPPPPPPPPPP

p pppppppppppppppppp
pppppppppppppppppp

Q QQQQQQQQQQQQQQQQQ
QQQQQQQQQQQQQQQQQ

q qqqqqqqqqqqqqqqqqqqq
qqqqqqqqqqqqqqqqqqq

R RRRRRRRRRRRRRRRRRR
RRRRRRRRRRRRRRRRRRR

r rrrrrrrrrrrrrrrrrrrr
rrrrrrrrrrrrrrrrrrrr

P P P P P P P P P P P P P P P P P P P

P P P P P P P P P P P P P P P P P P P

p p p p p p p p p p p p p p p p p p p

p p p p p p p p p p p p p p p p p p p

Q Q Q Q Q Q Q Q Q Q Q Q Q Q Q Q Q

Q Q Q Q Q Q Q Q Q Q Q Q Q Q Q Q Q Q

q q q q q q q q q q q q q q q q q q q q q

q q q q q q q q q q q q q q q q q q q q

R R R R R R R R R R R R R R R R R R R R

R R R R R R R R R R R R R R R R R R R R R

r r r r r r r r r r r r r r r r r r r r

r r r r r r r r r r r r r r r r r r r r

P P P P P P P P P P P P P P P P P P

P P P P P P P P P P P P P P P P P P

p p p p p p p p p p p p p p p p p p p

p p p p p p p p p p p p p p p p p p

Q Q Q Q Q Q Q Q Q Q Q Q Q Q Q Q Q Q

Q Q Q Q Q Q Q Q Q Q Q Q Q Q Q Q Q Q

q q q q q q q q q q q q q q q q q q q q

q q q q q q q q q q q q q q q q q q q

R R R R R R R R R R R R R R R R R R R

R R R R R R R R R R R R R R R R R R R R

r r r r r r r r r r r r r r r r r r r r

r r r r r r r r r r r r r r r r r r r r

P P P P P P P P P P P P P P P P P P P
P P P P P P P P P P P P P P P P P P P

p p p p p p p p p p p p p p p p p p p
p p p p p p p p p p p p p p p p p p p

Q Q Q Q Q Q Q Q Q Q Q Q Q Q Q
Q Q Q Q Q Q Q Q Q Q Q Q Q Q Q

q q q q q q q q q q q q q q q q q q q
q q q q q q q q q q q q q q q q q q q

R R R R R R R R R R R R R R R R R R R
R R R R R R R R R R R R R R R R R R R

r r r r r r r r r r r r r r r r r r r
r r r r r r r r r r r r r r r r r r r

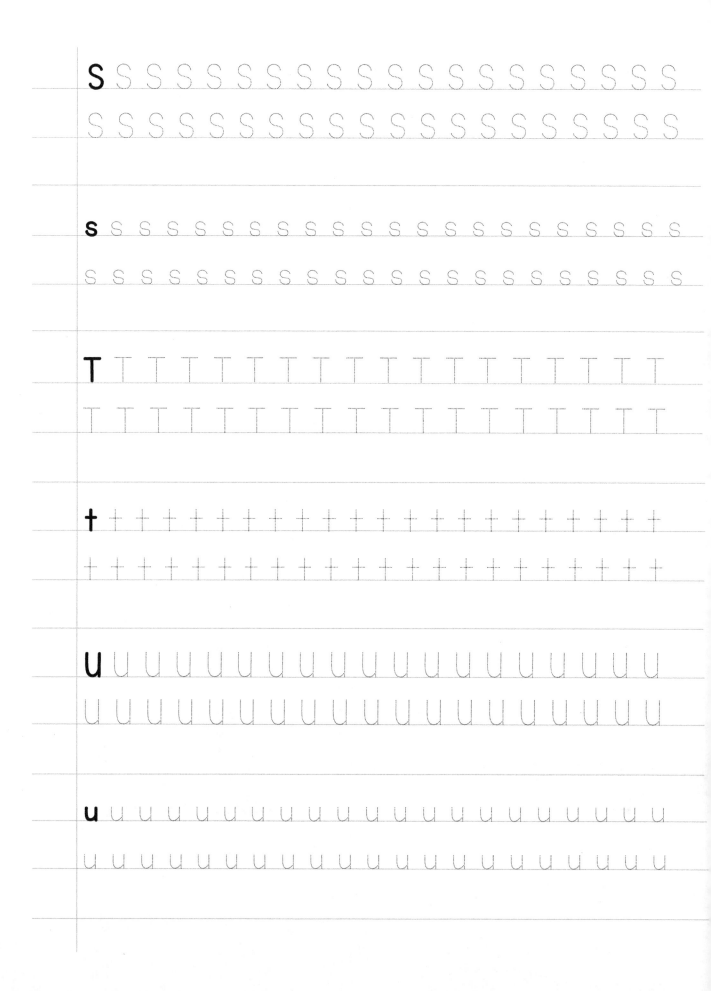

S S S S S S S S S S S S S S S S S S S

S S S S S S S S S S S S S S S S S S

s s s s s s s s s s s s s s s s s s s

s s s s s s s s s s s s s s s s s s s

T T T T T T T T T T T T T T T T T T T

T T T T T T T T T T T T T T T T T T T

t t t t t t t t t t t t t t t t t t t t

t t t t t t t t t t t t t t t t t t t t

u u u u u u u u u u u u u u u u u u u u

u u u u u u u u u u u u u u u u u u u u

u u u u u u u u u u u u u u u u u u u

u u u u u u u u u u u u u u u u u u u

S S S S S S S S S S S S S S S S S S S S S
S S S S S S S S S S S S S S S S S S S S

s s s s s s s s s s s s s s s s s s s s s
s s s s s s s s s s s s s s s s s s s s s

T T T T T T T T T T T T T T T T T T T T T
T T T T T T T T T T T T T T T T T T T T T

t t t t t t t t t t t t t t t t t t t t t
t t t t t t t t t t t t t t t t t t t t t

u u u u u u u u u u u u u u u u u u u u u
u u u u u u u u u u u u u u u u u u u u u

u u u u u u u u u u u u u u u u u u u u u
u u u u u u u u u u u u u u u u u u u u u

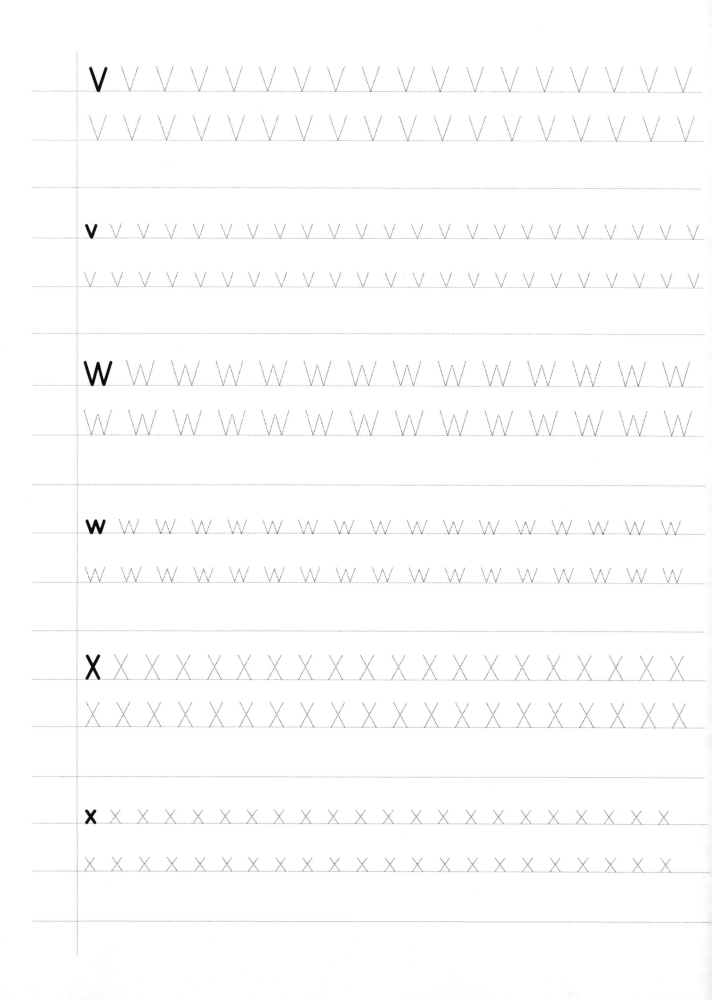

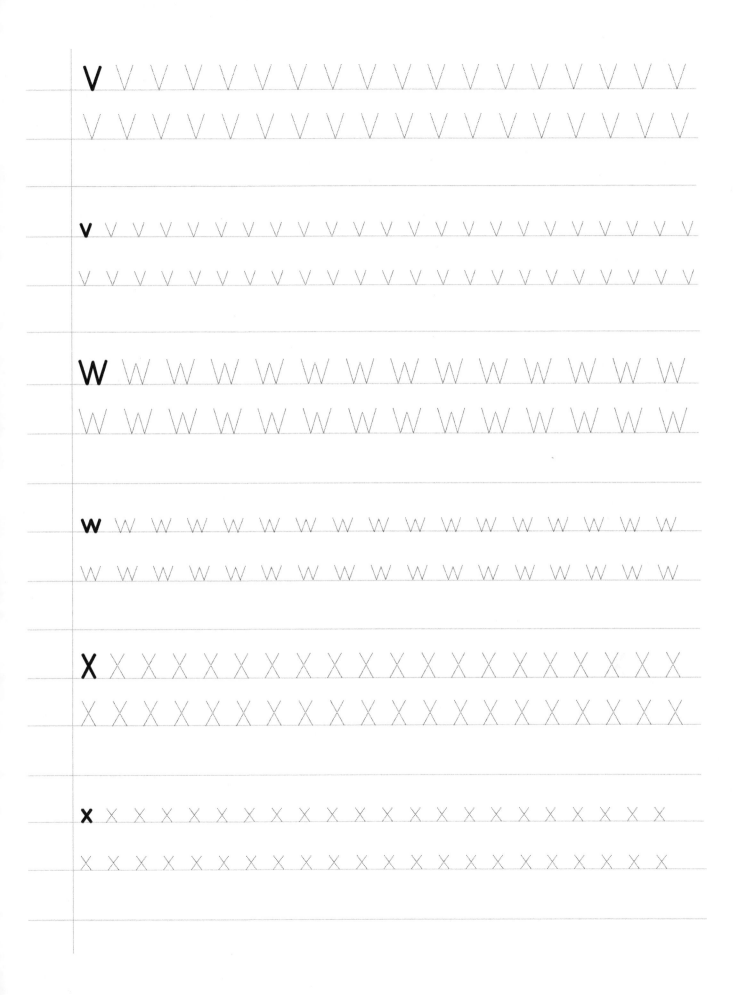

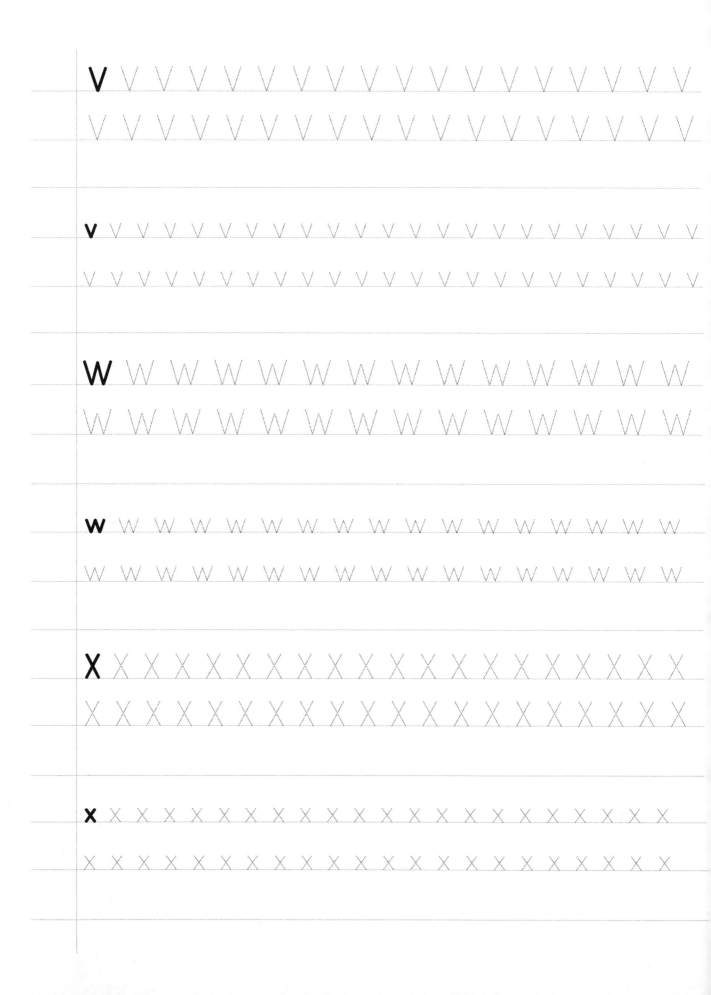

V V V V V V V V V V V V V V V V V
V V V V V V V V V V V V V V V V V

v v v v v v v v v v v v v v v v v v v
v v v v v v v v v v v v v v v v v v v

W W W W W W W W W W W W W
W W W W W W W W W W W W W W

w w w w w w w w w w w w w w w
w w w w w w w w w w w w w w w w

X X X X X X X X X X X X X X X
X X X X X X X X X X X X X X X

x x x x x x x x x x x x x x x x x x
x x x x x x x x x x x x x x x x x

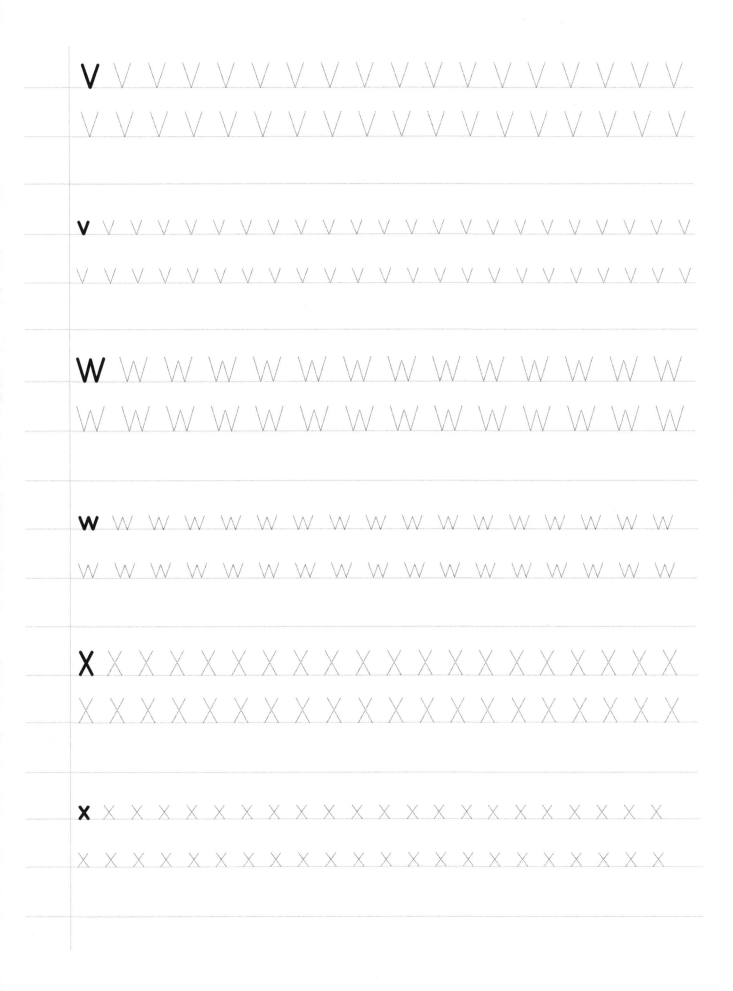

Y Y Y Y Y Y Y Y Y Y Y Y Y Y Y Y Y Y Y Y Y
Y Y Y Y Y Y Y Y Y Y Y Y Y Y Y Y Y Y Y Y Y
Y Y Y Y Y Y Y Y Y Y Y Y Y Y Y Y Y Y Y Y Y

y y y y y y y y y y y y y y y y y y y y y y
y y y y y y y y y y y y y y y y y y y y y y
y y y y y y y y y y y y y y y y y y y y y y

Z Z Z Z Z Z Z Z Z Z Z Z Z Z Z Z Z Z Z Z
Z Z Z Z Z Z Z Z Z Z Z Z Z Z Z Z Z Z Z Z
Z Z Z Z Z Z Z Z Z Z Z Z Z Z Z Z Z Z Z Z

z z z z z z z z z z z z z z z z z z z z z z
z z z z z z z z z z z z z z z z z z z z z z
z z z z z z z z z z z z z z z z z z z z z z

Y Y Y Y Y Y Y Y Y Y Y Y Y Y Y Y Y Y Y Y Y

Y Y Y Y Y Y Y Y Y Y Y Y Y Y Y Y Y Y Y Y Y

Y Y Y Y Y Y Y Y Y Y Y Y Y Y Y Y Y Y Y Y Y

y y y y y y y y y y y y y y y y y y y y y

y y y y y y y y y y y y y y y y y y y y y

y y y y y y y y y y y y y y y y y y y y y

Z Z Z Z Z Z Z Z Z Z Z Z Z Z Z Z Z Z Z Z

Z Z Z Z Z Z Z Z Z Z Z Z Z Z Z Z Z Z Z Z

Z Z Z Z Z Z Z Z Z Z Z Z Z Z Z Z Z Z Z Z

z z z z z z z z z z z z z z z z z z z z z z z

z z z z z z z z z z z z z z z z z z z z z z z

z z z z z z z z z z z z z z z z z z z z z z z

Airplane Airplane Airplane Airplane

Airplane Airplane Airplane Airplane

Airplane Airplane Airplane Airplane

Airplane Airplane Airplane Airplane

Astonish Astonish Astonish Astonish

Astonish Astonish Astonish Astonish

Astonish Astonish Astonish Astonish

Apple Apple Apple Apple Apple Apple

Apple Apple Apple Apple Apple Apple

Apple Apple Apple Apple Apple Apple

Apple Apple Apple Apple Apple Apple

Ambitious Ambitious Ambitious Ambitious

Ambitious Ambitious Ambitious Ambitious

Ambitious Ambitious Ambitious Ambitious

Acceptance Acceptance Acceptance
Acceptance Acceptance Acceptance
Acceptance Acceptance Acceptance
Acceptance Acceptance Acceptance

Alligator Alligator Alligator Alligator
Alligator Alligator Alligator Alligator
Alligator Alligator Alligator Alligator

Ability Ability Ability Ability Ability Ability
Ability Ability Ability Ability Ability Ability
Ability Ability Ability Ability Ability Ability
Ability Ability Ability Ability Ability Ability

Adventure Adventure Adventure
Adventure Adventure Adventure
Adventure Adventure Adventure

Brother Brother Brother Brother Brother
Brother Brother Brother Brother Brother
Brother Brother Brother Brother Brother
Brother Brother Brother Brother Brother

Blossom Blossom Blossom Blossom
Blossom Blossom Blossom Blossom
Blossom Blossom Blossom Blossom

Backup Backup Backup Backup Backup
Backup Backup Backup Backup Backup
Backup Backup Backup Backup Backup
Backup Backup Backup Backup Backup

Butterfly Butterfly Butterfly Butterfly
Butterfly Butterfly Butterfly Butterfly
Butterfly Butterfly Butterfly Butterfly

Barber Barber Barber Barber Barber
Barber Barber Barber Barber Barber
Barber Barber Barber Barber Barber
Barber Barber Barber Barber Barber

Bewilder Bewilder Bewilder Bewilder
Bewilder Bewilder Bewilder Bewilder
Bewilder Bewilder Bewilder Bewilder

Balance Balance Balance Balance Balance
Balance Balance Balance Balance Balance
Balance Balance Balance Balance Balance
Balance Balance Balance Balance Balance

Brilliant Brilliant Brilliant Brilliant Brilliant
Brilliant Brilliant Brilliant Brilliant Brilliant
Brilliant Brilliant Brilliant Brilliant Brilliant

Calculate Calculate Calculate Calculate

Calculate Calculate Calculate Calculate

Calculate Calculate Calculate Calculate

Calculate Calculate Calculate Calculate

Celebrate Celebrate Celebrate Celebrate

Celebrate Celebrate Celebrate Celebrate

Celebrate Celebrate Celebrate Celebrate

Capable Capable Capable Capable

Capable Capable Capable Capable Capable

Capable Capable Capable Capable Capable

Capable Capable Capable Capable Capable

Courageous Courageous Courageous

Courageous Courageous Courageous

Courageous Courageous Courageous

Camera Camera Camera Camera Camera
Camera Camera Camera Camera Camera
Camera Camera Camera Camera Camera
Camera Camera Camera Camera Camera

Captivate Captivate Captivate Captivate
Captivate Captivate Captivate Captivate
Captivate Captivate Captivate Captivate

Campaign Campaign Campaign Campaign
Campaign Campaign Campaign Campaign
Campaign Campaign Campaign Campaign
Campaign Campaign Campaign Campaign

Charismatic Charismatic Charismatic
Charismatic Charismatic Charismatic
Charismatic Charismatic Charismatic

Daily Daily Daily Daily Daily Daily Daily
Daily Daily Daily Daily Daily Daily Daily
Daily Daily Daily Daily Daily Daily Daily
Daily Daily Daily Daily Daily Daily Daily

Delightful Delightful Delightful Delightful
Delightful Delightful Delightful Delightful
Delightful Delightful Delightful Delightful

Decrease Decrease Decrease Decrease
Decrease Decrease Decrease Decrease
Decrease Decrease Decrease Decrease
Decrease Decrease Decrease Decrease

Determined Determined Determined
Determined Determined Determined
Determined Determined Determined

Decorative Decorative Decorative
Decorative Decorative Decorative
Decorative Decorative Decorative
Decorative Decorative Decorative

Dreamy Dreamy Dreamy Dreamy
Dreamy Dreamy Dreamy Dreamy
Dreamy Dreamy Dreamy Dreamy

Defeat Defeat Defeat Defeat Defeat
Defeat Defeat Defeat Defeat Defeat
Defeat Defeat Defeat Defeat Defeat
Defeat Defeat Defeat Defeat Defeat

Declined Declined Declined Declined
Declined Declined Declined Declined
Declined Declined Declined Declined

Early Early Early Early Early Early Early
Early Early Early Early Early Early Early
Early Early Early Early Early Early Early
Early Early Early Early Early Early Early

Eloquent Eloquent Eloquent Eloquent
Eloquent Eloquent Eloquent Eloquent
Eloquent Eloquent Eloquent Eloquent

Economist Economist Economist
Economist Economist Economist
Economist Economist Economist
Economist Economist Economist

Empathy Empathy Empathy Empathy
Empathy Empathy Empathy Empathy
Empathy Empathy Empathy Empathy

Educate Educate Educate Educate
Educate Educate Educate Educate
Educate Educate Educate Educate
Educate Educate Educate Educate

Energetic Energetic Energetic Energetic
Energetic Energetic Energetic Energetic
Energetic Energetic Energetic Energetic

Elastic Elastic Elastic Elastic Elastic
Elastic Elastic Elastic Elastic Elastic
Elastic Elastic Elastic Elastic Elastic
Elastic Elastic Elastic Elastic Elastic

Effervescent Effervescent Effervescent
Effervescent Effervescent Effervescent
Effervescent Effervescent Effervescent

Factory Factory Factory Factory Factory
Factory Factory Factory Factory Factory
Factory Factory Factory Factory Factory
Factory Factory Factory Factory Factory

Fantastic Fantastic Fantastic Fantastic
Fantastic Fantastic Fantastic Fantastic
Fantastic Fantastic Fantastic Fantastic

Familiar Familiar Familiar Familiar
Familiar Familiar Familiar Familiar
Familiar Familiar Familiar Familiar
Familiar Familiar Familiar Familiar

Friendly Friendly Friendly Friendly
Friendly Friendly Friendly Friendly
Friendly Friendly Friendly Friendly

Farmer Farmer Farmer Farmer Farmer
Farmer Farmer Farmer Farmer Farmer
Farmer Farmer Farmer Farmer Farmer
Farmer Farmer Farmer Farmer Farmer

Fragrant Fragrant Fragrant Fragrant
Fragrant Fragrant Fragrant Fragrant
Fragrant Fragrant Fragrant Fragrant

Female Female Female Female Female
Female Female Female Female Female
Female Female Female Female Female
Female Female Female Female Female

Fulfillment Fulfillment Fulfillment
Fulfillment Fulfillment Fulfillment
Fulfillment Fulfillment Fulfillment

Generous Generous Generous Generous
Generous Generous Generous Generous
Generous Generous Generous Generous
Generous Generous Generous Generous

Grateful Grateful Grateful Grateful
Grateful Grateful Grateful Grateful
Grateful Grateful Grateful Grateful

Global Global Global Global Global Global
Global Global Global Global Global Global
Global Global Global Global Global Global
Global Global Global Global Global Global

Gourmet Gourmet Gourmet Gourmet
Gourmet Gourmet Gourmet Gourmet
Gourmet Gourmet Gourmet Gourmet

Golden Golden Golden

Golden Golden Golden

Golden Golden Golden

Golden Golden Golden

Glorious Glorious Glorious Glorious

Glorious Glorious Glorious Glorious

Glorious Glorious Glorious Glorious

Graduate Graduate Graduate Graduate

Graduate Graduate Graduate Graduate

Graduate Graduate Graduate Graduate

Graduate Graduate Graduate Graduate

Gigantic Gigantic Gigantic Gigantic

Gigantic Gigantic Gigantic Gigantic

Gigantic Gigantic Gigantic Gigantic

Handle Handle Handle Handle Handle
Handle Handle Handle Handle Handle
Handle Handle Handle Handle Handle
Handle Handle Handle Handle Handle

Humble Humble Humble Humble Humble
Humble Humble Humble Humble Humble
Humble Humble Humble Humble Humble

Happy Happy Happy Happy Happy Happy
Happy Happy Happy Happy Happy Happy
Happy Happy Happy Happy Happy Happy
Happy Happy Happy Happy Happy Happy

Hilarious Hilarious Hilarious Hilarious
Hilarious Hilarious Hilarious Hilarious
Hilarious Hilarious Hilarious Hilarious

Headache Headache Headache Headache
Headache Headache Headache Headache
Headache Headache Headache Headache
Headache Headache Headache Headache

Harmony Harmony Harmony Harmony
Harmony Harmony Harmony Harmony
Harmony Harmony Harmony Harmony

Health Health Health Health Health
Health Health Health Health Health Health
Health Health Health Health Health Health
Health Health Health Health Health Health

Hopeful Hopeful Hopeful Hopeful Hopeful
Hopeful Hopeful Hopeful Hopeful Hopeful
Hopeful Hopeful Hopeful Hopeful Hopeful

Identical Identical Identical Identical Identical Identical Identical Identical Identical Identical Identical Identical Identical Identical Identical Identical Identical

Incredible Incredible Incredible Incredible Incredible Incredible Incredible Incredible Incredible

Ignore Ignore Ignore Ignore Ignore Ignore Ignore Ignore Ignore Ignore Ignore Ignore Ignore Ignore Ignore Ignore Ignore Ignore Ignore

Immaculate Immaculate Immaculate Immaculate Immaculate Immaculate Immaculate Immaculate Immaculate

Immediate Immediate Immediate
Immediate Immediate Immediate
Immediate Immediate Immediate
Immediate Immediate Immediate

Impressive Impressive Impressive
Impressive Impressive Impressive
Impressive Impressive Impressive

Impact Impact Impact Impact Impact
Impact Impact Impact Impact Impact
Impact Impact Impact Impact Impact
Impact Impact Impact Impact Impact

Indulgent Indulgent Indulgent Indulgent
Indulgent Indulgent Indulgent Indulgent
Indulgent Indulgent Indulgent Indulgent

Jacket Jacket Jacket Jacket Jacket
Jacket Jacket Jacket Jacket Jacket
Jacket Jacket Jacket Jacket Jacket
Jacket Jacket Jacket Jacket Jacket

Justify Justify Justify Justify Justify
Justify Justify Justify Justify Justify
Justify Justify Justify Justify Justify

Journey Journey Journey Journey
Journey Journey Journey Journey
Journey Journey Journey Journey
Journey Journey Journey Journey

Juxtapose Juxtapose Juxtapose
Juxtapose Juxtapose Juxtapose
Juxtapose Juxtapose Juxtapose

Judge Judge Judge Judge Judge Judge
Judge Judge Judge Judge Judge Judge
Judge Judge Judge Judge Judge Judge
Judge Judge Judge Judge Judge Judge

Jamboree Jamboree Jamboree Jamboree
Jamboree Jamboree Jamboree Jamboree
Jamboree Jamboree Jamboree Jamboree

Junior Junior Junior Junior Junior
Junior Junior Junior Junior Junior
Junior Junior Junior Junior Junior
Junior Junior Junior Junior Junior

Jovial Jovial Jovial Jovial Jovial Jovial
Jovial Jovial Jovial Jovial Jovial Jovial
Jovial Jovial Jovial Jovial Jovial Jovial

Kindness Kindness Kindness Kindness
Kindness Kindness Kindness Kindness
Kindness Kindness Kindness Kindness
Kindness Kindness Kindness Kindness

Karaoke Karaoke Karaoke Karaoke
Karaoke Karaoke Karaoke Karaoke
Karaoke Karaoke Karaoke Karaoke

Knowledge Knowledge Knowledge
Knowledge Knowledge Knowledge
Knowledge Knowledge Knowledge
Knowledge Knowledge Knowledge

Ketchup Ketchup Ketchup Ketchup
Ketchup Ketchup Ketchup Ketchup
Ketchup Ketchup Ketchup Ketchup

Kingdom Kingdom Kingdom Kingdom
Kingdom Kingdom Kingdom Kingdom
Kingdom Kingdom Kingdom Kingdom
Kingdom Kingdom Kingdom Kingdom

Keystone Keystone Keystone Keystone
Keystone Keystone Keystone Keystone
Keystone Keystone Keystone Keystone

Knock Knock Knock Knock Knock
Knock Knock Knock Knock Knock
Knock Knock Knock Knock Knock
Knock Knock Knock Knock Knock

Koala Koala Koala Koala Koala Koala
Koala Koala Koala Koala Koala Koala
Koala Koala Koala Koala Koala Koala

Laboratory Laboratory Laboratory Laboratory Laboratory Laboratory Laboratory Laboratory Laboratory Laboratory

Lovely Lovely Lovely Lovely Lovely Lovely Lovely Lovely Lovely Lovely Lovely Lovely Lovely Lovely Lovely Lovely Lovely Lovely

Landing Landing Landing Landing Landing Landing Landing Landing Landing Landing Landing Landing Landing Landing Landing Landing Landing Landing Landing Landing

Legacy Legacy Legacy Legacy Legacy Legacy Legacy Legacy Legacy Legacy Legacy Legacy Legacy Legacy Legacy Legacy

Launch Launch Launch Launch
Launch Launch Launch Launch
Launch Launch Launch Launch
Launch Launch Launch Launch

Luxurious Luxurious Luxurious Luxurious
Luxurious Luxurious Luxurious Luxurious
Luxurious Luxurious Luxurious Luxurious

League League League League League
League League League League League
League League League League League
League League League League League

Leisure Leisure Leisure Leisure Leisure
Leisure Leisure Leisure Leisure Leisure
Leisure Leisure Leisure Leisure Leisure

Magazine Magazine Magazine Magazine
Magazine Magazine Magazine Magazine
Magazine Magazine Magazine Magazine
Magazine Magazine Magazine Magazine

Motivated Motivated Motivated Motivated
Motivated Motivated Motivated Motivated
Motivated Motivated Motivated Motivated

Management Management Management
Management Management Management
Management Management Management
Management Management Management

Momentum Momentum Momentum
Momentum Momentum Momentum
Momentum Momentum Momentum

Manner Manner Manner Manner Manner
Manner Manner Manner Manner Manner
Manner Manner Manner Manner Manner
Manner Manner Manner Manner Manner

Melodious Melodious Melodious Melodious
Melodious Melodious Melodious Melodious
Melodious Melodious Melodious Melodious

Manufacture Manufacture Manufacture
Manufacture Manufacture Manufacture
Manufacture Manufacture Manufacture
Manufacture Manufacture Manufacture

Mystic Mystic Mystic Mystic Mystic
Mystic Mystic Mystic Mystic Mystic
Mystic Mystic Mystic Mystic Mystic

Naturally Naturally Naturally Naturally
Naturally Naturally Naturally Naturally
Naturally Naturally Naturally Naturally
Naturally Naturally Naturally Naturally

Nuanced Nuanced Nuanced
Nuanced Nuanced Nuanced
Nuanced Nuanced Nuanced

Necessary Necessary Necessary
Necessary Necessary Necessary
Necessary Necessary Necessary
Necessary Necessary Necessary

Nurturing Nurturing Nurturing Nurturing
Nurturing Nurturing Nurturing Nurturing
Nurturing Nurturing Nurturing Nurturing

Neighbor Neighbor Neighbor Neighbor
Neighbor Neighbor Neighbor Neighbor
Neighbor Neighbor Neighbor Neighbor
Neighbor Neighbor Neighbor Neighbor

Noteworthy Noteworthy Noteworthy
Noteworthy Noteworthy Noteworthy
Noteworthy Noteworthy Noteworthy

Network Network Network Network
Network Network Network Network
Network Network Network Network
Network Network Network Network

Novel Novel Novel Novel Novel Novel Novel
Novel Novel Novel Novel Novel Novel Novel
Novel Novel Novel Novel Novel Novel Novel

Obtain Obtain Obtain Obtain Obtain Obtain
Obtain Obtain Obtain Obtain Obtain Obtain
Obtain Obtain Obtain Obtain Obtain Obtain
Obtain Obtain Obtain Obtain Obtain Obtain

Optimistic Optimistic Optimistic Optimistic
Optimistic Optimistic Optimistic Optimistic
Optimistic Optimistic Optimistic Optimistic

Occasionally Occasionally Occasionally
Occasionally Occasionally Occasionally
Occasionally Occasionally Occasionally
Occasionally Occasionally Occasionally

Oasis Oasis Oasis Oasis Oasis Oasis
Oasis Oasis Oasis Oasis Oasis Oasis
Oasis Oasis Oasis Oasis Oasis Oasis

Objective Objective Objective Objective Objective Objective Objective Objective Objective Objective Objective Objective Objective Objective

Outstanding Outstanding Outstanding Outstanding Outstanding Outstanding Outstanding Outstanding Outstanding

Officer Officer

Overcome Overcome Overcome Overcome Overcome Overcome Overcome Overcome Overcome Overcome Overcome Overcome

Package Package Package Package
Package Package Package Package
Package Package Package Package
Package Package Package Package

Passionate Passionate Passionate
Passionate Passionate Passionate
Passionate Passionate Passionate

Painting Painting Painting Painting Painting
Painting Painting Painting Painting Painting
Painting Painting Painting Painting Painting
Painting Painting Painting Painting Painting

Peaceful Peaceful Peaceful Peaceful
Peaceful Peaceful Peaceful Peaceful
Peaceful Peaceful Peaceful Peaceful

Parent Parent Parent Parent Parent Parent
Parent Parent Parent Parent Parent Parent
Parent Parent Parent Parent Parent Parent
Parent Parent Parent Parent Parent Parent

Perseverance Perseverance Perseverance
Perseverance Perseverance Perseverance
Perseverance Perseverance Perseverance

Paragraph Paragraph Paragraph
Paragraph Paragraph Paragraph
Paragraph Paragraph Paragraph
Paragraph Paragraph Paragraph

Prosperous Prosperous Prosperous
Prosperous Prosperous Prosperous
Prosperous Prosperous Prosperous

Quantity Quantity Quantity Quantity
Quantity Quantity Quantity Quantity
Quantity Quantity Quantity Quantity
Quantity Quantity Quantity Quantity

Quality Quality Quality Quality Quality
Quality Quality Quality Quality Quality
Quality Quality Quality Quality Quality

Qualification Qualification Qualification
Qualification Qualification Qualification
Qualification Qualification Qualification
Qualification Qualification Qualification

Quiet Quiet Quiet Quiet Quiet Quiet Quiet
Quiet Quiet Quiet Quiet Quiet Quiet Quiet
Quiet Quiet Quiet Quiet Quiet Quiet Quiet

Queen Queen Queen Queen Queen Queen
Queen Queen Queen Queen Queen Queen
Queen Queen Queen Queen Queen Queen
Queen Queen Queen Queen Queen Queen

Quaint Quaint Quaint Quaint Quaint Quaint
Quaint Quaint Quaint Quaint Quaint Quaint
Quaint Quaint Quaint Quaint Quaint Quaint

Quick Quick Quick Quick Quick Quick Quick
Quick Quick Quick Quick Quick Quick Quick
Quick Quick Quick Quick Quick Quick Quick
Quick Quick Quick Quick Quick Quick Quick

Quench Quench Quench Quench Quench
Quench Quench Quench Quench Quench
Quench Quench Quench Quench Quench

Radiation Radiation Radiation Radiation
Radiation Radiation Radiation Radiation
Radiation Radiation Radiation Radiation
Radiation Radiation Radiation Radiation

Remarkable Remarkable Remarkable
Remarkable Remarkable Remarkable
Remarkable Remarkable Remarkable

Rather Rather Rather Rather Rather
Rather Rather Rather Rather Rather
Rather Rather Rather Rather Rather
Rather Rather Rather Rather Rather

Refreshing Refreshing Refreshing
Refreshing Refreshing Refreshing
Refreshing Refreshing Refreshing

Reach Reach Reach Reach Reach Reach
Reach Reach Reach Reach Reach Reach
Reach Reach Reach Reach Reach Reach
Reach Reach Reach Reach Reach Reach

Relentless Relentless Relentless Relentless
Relentless Relentless Relentless Relentless
Relentless Relentless Relentless Relentless

Reading Reading Reading Reading Reading
Reading Reading Reading Reading Reading
Reading Reading Reading Reading Reading
Reading Reading Reading Reading Reading

Resourceful Resourceful Resourceful
Resourceful Resourceful Resourceful
Resourceful Resourceful Resourceful

Safety Safety Safety Safety Safety
Safety Safety Safety Safety Safety
Safety Safety Safety Safety Safety
Safety Safety Safety Safety Safety

Spectacular Spectacular Spectacular
Spectacular Spectacular Spectacular
Spectacular Spectacular Spectacular

Sandwich Sandwich Sandwich Sandwich
Sandwich Sandwich Sandwich Sandwich
Sandwich Sandwich Sandwich Sandwich
Sandwich Sandwich Sandwich Sandwich

Sincere Sincere Sincere Sincere Sincere
Sincere Sincere Sincere Sincere Sincere
Sincere Sincere Sincere Sincere Sincere

Satisfaction Satisfaction Satisfaction
Satisfaction Satisfaction Satisfaction
Satisfaction Satisfaction Satisfaction
Satisfaction Satisfaction Satisfaction

Splendid Splendid Splendid Splendid
Splendid Splendid Splendid Splendid
Splendid Splendid Splendid Splendid

Savings Savings Savings Savings Savings
Savings Savings Savings Savings Savings
Savings Savings Savings Savings Savings
Savings Savings Savings Savings Savings

Sunshine Sunshine Sunshine Sunshine
Sunshine Sunshine Sunshine Sunshine
Sunshine Sunshine Sunshine Sunshine

Target Target Target Target Target
Target Target Target Target Target
Target Target Target Target Target
Target Target Target Target Target

Tranquil Tranquil Tranquil Tranquil
Tranquil Tranquil Tranquil Tranquil
Tranquil Tranquil Tranquil Tranquil

Teacher Teacher Teacher Teacher
Teacher Teacher Teacher Teacher
Teacher Teacher Teacher Teacher
Teacher Teacher Teacher Teacher

Treasure Treasure Treasure Treasure
Treasure Treasure Treasure Treasure
Treasure Treasure Treasure Treasure

Teammate Teammate Teammate
Teammate Teammate Teammate
Teammate Teammate Teammate
Teammate Teammate Teammate

Tenacious Tenacious Tenacious Tenacious
Tenacious Tenacious Tenacious Tenacious
Tenacious Tenacious Tenacious Tenacious

Technical Technical Technical Technical
Technical Technical Technical Technical
Technical Technical Technical Technical
Technical Technical Technical Technical

Triumph Triumph Triumph Triumph
Triumph Triumph Triumph Triumph
Triumph Triumph Triumph Triumph

Umbrella Umbrella Umbrella Umbrella
Umbrella Umbrella Umbrella Umbrella
Umbrella Umbrella Umbrella Umbrella
Umbrella Umbrella Umbrella Umbrella

Unforgettable Unforgettable
Unforgettable Unforgettable
Unforgettable Unforgettable

Uncle Uncle Uncle Uncle Uncle Uncle Uncle
Uncle Uncle Uncle Uncle Uncle Uncle Uncle
Uncle Uncle Uncle Uncle Uncle Uncle Uncle
Uncle Uncle Uncle Uncle Uncle Uncle Uncle

Unconditional Unconditional Unconditional
Unconditional Unconditional Unconditional
Unconditional Unconditional Unconditional

Unique Unique Unique Unique Unique
Unique Unique Unique Unique Unique
Unique Unique Unique Unique Unique
Unique Unique Unique Unique Unique

Ultimate Ultimate Ultimate Ultimate
Ultimate Ultimate Ultimate Ultimate
Ultimate Ultimate Ultimate Ultimate

Universal Universal Universal Universal
Universal Universal Universal Universal
Universal Universal Universal Universal
Universal Universal Universal Universal

Unwavering Unwavering Unwavering
Unwavering Unwavering Unwavering
Unwavering Unwavering Unwavering

Vacation Vacation Vacation Vacation
Vacation Vacation Vacation Vacation
Vacation Vacation Vacation Vacation
Vacation Vacation Vacation Vacation

Victory Victory Victory Victory Victory
Victory Victory Victory Victory Victory
Victory Victory Victory Victory Victory

Variety Variety Variety Variety Variety
Variety Variety Variety Variety Variety
Variety Variety Variety Variety Variety
Variety Variety Variety Variety Variety

Vitality Vitality Vitality Vitality Vitality
Vitality Vitality Vitality Vitality Vitality
Vitality Vitality Vitality Vitality Vitality

Vegetable Vegetable Vegetable Vegetable
Vegetable Vegetable Vegetable Vegetable
Vegetable Vegetable Vegetable Vegetable
Vegetable Vegetable Vegetable Vegetable

Valiant Valiant Valiant Valiant
Valiant Valiant Valiant Valiant Valiant
Valiant Valiant Valiant Valiant Valiant

Version Version Version Version
Version Version Version Version Version
Version Version Version Version Version
Version Version Version Version Version

Vigorous Vigorous Vigorous Vigorous
Vigorous Vigorous Vigorous Vigorous
Vigorous Vigorous Vigorous Vigorous

Waiting Waiting Waiting Waiting Waiting
Waiting Waiting Waiting Waiting Waiting
Waiting Waiting Waiting Waiting Waiting
Waiting Waiting Waiting Waiting Waiting

Windsurf Windsurf Windsurf Windsurf
Windsurf Windsurf Windsurf Windsurf
Windsurf Windsurf Windsurf Windsurf

Watching Watching Watching Watching
Watching Watching Watching Watching
Watching Watching Watching Watching
Watching Watching Watching Watching

Washington Washington Washington
Washington Washington Washington
Washington Washington Washington

Water Water Water Water Water
Water Water Water Water Water
Water Water Water Water Water
Water Water Water Water Water

Wanderlust Wanderlust Wanderlust
Wanderlust Wanderlust Wanderlust
Wanderlust Wanderlust Wanderlust

Welcome Welcome Welcome Welcome
Welcome Welcome Welcome Welcome
Welcome Welcome Welcome Welcome
Welcome Welcome Welcome Welcome

Wholesome Wholesome Wholesome
Wholesome Wholesome Wholesome
Wholesome Wholesome Wholesome

Xylophone Xylophone Xylophone Xylophone
Xylophone Xylophone Xylophone Xylophone
Xylophone Xylophone Xylophone Xylophone
Xylophone Xylophone Xylophone Xylophone
Xylophone Xylophone Xylophone Xylophone
Xylophone Xylophone Xylophone Xylophone

Xerography Xerography Xerography
Xerography Xerography Xerography
Xerography Xerography Xerography
Xerography Xerography Xerography
Xerography Xerography Xerography
Xerography Xerography Xerography

X-ray X-ray X-ray X-ray X-ray X-ray
X-ray X-ray X-ray X-ray X-ray X-ray
X-ray X-ray X-ray X-ray X-ray X-ray
X-ray X-ray X-ray X-ray X-ray X-ray
X-ray X-ray X-ray X-ray X-ray X-ray
X-ray X-ray X-ray X-ray X-ray X-ray

Xylography Xylography Xylography
Xylography Xylography Xylography
Xylography Xylography Xylography
Xylography Xylography Xylography
Xylography Xylography Xylography
Xylography Xylography Xylography

Young Young

Youthful Youthful Youthful Youthful Youthful Youthful Youthful Youthful Youthful Youthful Youthful Youthful Youthful

Yourself Yourself Yourself Yourself Yourself Yourself Yourself Yourself Yourself Yourself Yourself Yourself

Yield Yield

Years Years Years Years Years Years
Years Years Years Years Years Years
Years Years Years Years Years Years
Years Years Years Years Years Years

Yonder Yonder Yonder Yonder Yonder
Yonder Yonder Yonder Yonder Yonder
Yonder Yonder Yonder Yonder Yonder

Yesterday Yesterday Yesterday
Yesterday Yesterday Yesterday
Yesterday Yesterday Yesterday
Yesterday Yesterday Yesterday

Yarn Yarn Yarn Yarn Yarn Yarn Yarn
Yarn Yarn Yarn Yarn Yarn Yarn Yarn
Yarn Yarn Yarn Yarn Yarn Yarn Yarn

Zero Zero Zero Zero Zero Zero Zero
Zero Zero Zero Zero Zero Zero Zero
Zero Zero Zero Zero Zero Zero Zero
Zero Zero Zero Zero Zero Zero Zero

Zesty Zesty Zesty Zesty Zesty Zesty
Zesty Zesty Zesty Zesty Zesty Zesty
Zesty Zesty Zesty Zesty Zesty Zesty

Zone Zone Zone Zone Zone Zone Zone
Zone Zone Zone Zone Zone Zone Zone
Zone Zone Zone Zone Zone Zone Zone
Zone Zone Zone Zone Zone Zone Zone

Zenith Zenith Zenith Zenith Zenith Zenith
Zenith Zenith Zenith Zenith Zenith Zenith
Zenith Zenith Zenith Zenith Zenith Zenith

Zipper Zipper Zipper Zipper Zipper Zipper
Zipper Zipper Zipper Zipper Zipper Zipper
Zipper Zipper Zipper Zipper Zipper Zipper
Zipper Zipper Zipper Zipper Zipper Zipper

Zealous Zealous Zealous Zealous Zealous
Zealous Zealous Zealous Zealous Zealous
Zealous Zealous Zealous Zealous Zealous

Zebra Zebra Zebra Zebra Zebra Zebra
Zebra Zebra Zebra Zebra Zebra Zebra
Zebra Zebra Zebra Zebra Zebra Zebra
Zebra Zebra Zebra Zebra Zebra Zebra

Zigzag Zigzag Zigzag Zigzag Zigzag
Zigzag Zigzag Zigzag Zigzag Zigzag
Zigzag Zigzag Zigzag Zigzag Zigzag

Your dreams can come true, trust in yourself all you need is to work

Your dreams can come true, trust in yourself
all you need is to work

Your dreams can come true, trust in yourself
all you need is to work

Your dreams can come true, trust in yourself
all you need is to work

Your dreams can come true, trust in yourself
all you need is to work

Your dreams can come true, trust in yourself
all you need is to work

Your dreams can come true, trust in yourself
all you need is to work

Your dreams can come true, trust in yourself
all you need is to work

Your dreams can come true, trust in yourself
all you need is to work

Take the path to success, don't limit yourself and don't let your dreams be just dreams

Take the path to success, don't limit yourself

and don't let your dreams be just dreams

Take the path to success, don't limit yourself

and don't let your dreams be just dreams

Take the path to success, don't limit yourself

and don't let your dreams be just dreams

Take the path to success, don't limit yourself

and don't let your dreams be just dreams

Take the path to success, don't limit yourself

and don't let your dreams be just dreams

Take the path to success, don't limit yourself

and don't let your dreams be just dreams

Take the path to success, don't limit yourself

and don't let your dreams be just dreams

Take the path to success, don't limit yourself

and don't let your dreams be just dreams

Never give up, and you will get there,
and have patience in the face of difficulties

Never give up, and you will get there,

and have patience in the face of difficulties

Never give up, and you will get there,

and have patience in the face of difficulties

Never give up, and you will get there,

and have patience in the face of difficulties

Never give up, and you will get there,

and have patience in the face of difficulties

Never give up, and you will get there,

and have patience in the face of difficulties

Never give up, and you will get there,

and have patience in the face of difficulties

Never give up, and you will get there,

and have patience in the face of difficulties

Your imagination will guide you towards your
goals, if you can dream it, you can achieve it

Your imagination will guide you towards your
goals, if you can dream it, you can achieve it
Your imagination will guide you towards your
goals, if you can dream it, you can achieve it
Your imagination will guide you towards your
goals, if you can dream it, you can achieve it
Your imagination will guide you towards your
goals, if you can dream it, you can achieve it
Your imagination will guide you towards your
goals, if you can dream it, you can achieve it
Your imagination will guide you towards your
goals, if you can dream it, you can achieve it

Always be kind to those around you and surround yourself with positivity and ambition

Always be kind to those around you and
surround yourself with positivity and ambition
Always be kind to those around you and
surround yourself with positivity and ambition
Always be kind to those around you and
surround yourself with positivity and ambition
Always be kind to those around you and
surround yourself with positivity and ambition
Always be kind to those around you and
surround yourself with positivity and ambition
Always be kind to those around you and
surround yourself with positivity and ambition

There are two pains: success and regret, choose the right path

There are two pains: success and regret,
choose the right path

There are two pains: success and regret,
choose the right path

There are two pains: success and regret,
choose the right path

There are two pains: success and regret,
choose the right path

There are two pains: success and regret,
choose the right path

There are two pains: success and regret,
choose the right path

No matter how much you fail, try to get up, seek excellence, and success will follow

No matter how much you fail, try to get up,

seek excellence, and success will follow

No matter how much you fail, try to get up,

seek excellence, and success will follow

No matter how much you fail, try to get up,

seek excellence, and success will follow

No matter how much you fail, try to get up,

seek excellence, and success will follow

No matter how much you fail, try to get up,

seek excellence, and success will follow

No matter how much you fail, try to get up,

seek excellence, and success will follow

No matter how much you fail, try to get up,

seek excellence, and success will follow

No matter how much you fail, try to get up,

seek excellence, and success will follow

Believe in yourself and you can do anything, confidence is the secret to success

Believe in yourself and you can do anything, confidence is the secret to success

Believe in yourself and you can do anything, confidence is the secret to success

Believe in yourself and you can do anything, confidence is the secret to success

Believe in yourself and you can do anything, confidence is the secret to success

Believe in yourself and you can do anything, confidence is the secret to success

Believe in yourself and you can do anything, confidence is the secret to success

Believe in yourself and you can do anything, confidence is the secret to success

Believe in yourself and you can do anything, confidence is the secret to success

Don't be afraid to live new adventures, dare to step out of your comfort zone

Don't be afraid to live new adventures, dare
to step out of your comfort zone

Don't be afraid to live new adventures, dare
to step out of your comfort zone

Don't be afraid to live new adventures, dare
to step out of your comfort zone

Don't be afraid to live new adventures, dare
to step out of your comfort zone

Don't be afraid to live new adventures, dare
to step out of your comfort zone

Don't be afraid to live new adventures, dare
to step out of your comfort zone

Don't be afraid to live new adventures, dare
to step out of your comfort zone

Don't be afraid to live new adventures, dare
to step out of your comfort zone

Work hard to achieve your goals,
perseverance is the key to success

Work hard to achieve your goals,

perseverance is the key to success

Work hard to achieve your goals,

perseverance is the key to success

Work hard to achieve your goals,

perseverance is the key to success

Work hard to achieve your goals,

perseverance is the key to success

Work hard to achieve your goals,

perseverance is the key to success

Work hard to achieve your goals,

perseverance is the key to success

Learn from your failure and keep working, don't look back, you're not going that way

Learn from your failure and keep working,

don't look back, you're not going that way

Learn from your failure and keep working,

don't look back, you're not going that way

Learn from your failure and keep working,

don't look back, you're not going that way

Learn from your failure and keep working,

don't look back, you're not going that way

Learn from your failure and keep working,

don't look back, you're not going that way

Difficult days will strengthen you, life is 10%.
what happens to us and 90%. how we react

Difficult days will strengthen you, life is 10%.
what happens to us and 90%. how we react
Difficult days will strengthen you, life is 10%.
what happens to us and 90%. how we react
Difficult days will strengthen you, life is 10%.
what happens to us and 90%. how we react
Difficult days will strengthen you, life is 10%.
what happens to us and 90%. how we react
Difficult days will strengthen you, life is 10%.
what happens to us and 90%. how we react
Difficult days will strengthen you, life is 10%.
what happens to us and 90%. how we react

Don't let your fears affect you, motivation drives you and habits keep you

Don't let your fears affect you, motivation
drives you and habits keep you

Don't let your fears affect you, motivation
drives you and habits keep you

Don't let your fears affect you, motivation
drives you and habits keep you

Don't let your fears affect you, motivation
drives you and habits keep you

Don't let your fears affect you, motivation
drives you and habits keep you

Don't let your fears affect you, motivation
drives you and habits keep you

Try to make the right decision, there is no
better investment than investing in yourself

Try to make the right decision, there is no
better investment than investing in yourself
Try to make the right decision, there is no
better investment than investing in yourself
Try to make the right decision, there is no
better investment than investing in yourself
Try to make the right decision, there is no
better investment than investing in yourself
Try to make the right decision, there is no
better investment than investing in yourself
Try to make the right decision, there is no
better investment than investing in yourself

Work on your goals with passion, to do great work, love what you do

Work on your goals with passion, to do
great work, love what you do

Work on your goals with passion, to do
great work, love what you do

Work on your goals with passion, to do
great work, love what you do

Work on your goals with passion, to do
great work, love what you do

Work on your goals with passion, to do
great work, love what you do

Work on your goals with passion, to do
great work, love what you do

Be brave and face new challenges, discipline
is the bridge between goals and achievements

Be brave and face new challenges, discipline

is the bridge between goals and achievements

Be brave and face new challenges, discipline

is the bridge between goals and achievements

Be brave and face new challenges, discipline

is the bridge between goals and achievements

Be brave and face new challenges, discipline

is the bridge between goals and achievements

Be brave and face new challenges, discipline

is the bridge between goals and achievements

Be brave and face new challenges, discipline

is the bridge between goals and achievements

Be brave and face new challenges, discipline

is the bridge between goals and achievements

Be grateful and learn from your mistakes,
excuses will not bring you closer to your goals

Be grateful and learn from your mistakes,

excuses will not bring you closer to your goals

Be grateful and learn from your mistakes,

excuses will not bring you closer to your goals

Be grateful and learn from your mistakes,

excuses will not bring you closer to your goals

Be grateful and learn from your mistakes,

excuses will not bring you closer to your goals

Be grateful and learn from your mistakes,

excuses will not bring you closer to your goals

Start first and don't give up, the key to success is to start before you're ready

Start first and don't give up, the key to

success is to start before you're ready

Start first and don't give up, the key to

success is to start before you're ready

Start first and don't give up, the key to

success is to start before you're ready

Start first and don't give up, the key to

success is to start before you're ready

Start first and don't give up, the key to

success is to start before you're ready

Start first and don't give up, the key to

success is to start before you're ready

Believe in yourself, you are not what you have achieved, you are what you have overcome

Believe in yourself, you are not what you have
achieved, you are what you have overcome

Believe in yourself, you are not what you have
achieved, you are what you have overcome

Believe in yourself, you are not what you have
achieved, you are what you have overcome

Believe in yourself, you are not what you have
achieved, you are what you have overcome

Believe in yourself, you are not what you have
achieved, you are what you have overcome

Believe in yourself, you are not what you have
achieved, you are what you have overcome

Doubts are worse than failures, the mind is everything, what you think, you become

Doubts are worse than failures, the mind is
everything, what you think, you become
Doubts are worse than failures, the mind is
everything, what you think, you become
Doubts are worse than failures, the mind is
everything, what you think, you become
Doubts are worse than failures, the mind is
everything, what you think, you become
Doubts are worse than failures, the mind is
everything, what you think, you become
Doubts are worse than failures, the mind is
everything, what you think, you become

Every failure is a lesson, it's never too late to be who you could have been

Every failure is a lesson, it's never too late
to be who you could have been

Every failure is a lesson, it's never too late
to be who you could have been

Every failure is a lesson, it's never too late
to be who you could have been

Every failure is a lesson, it's never too late
to be who you could have been

Every failure is a lesson, it's never too late
to be who you could have been

Every failure is a lesson, it's never too late
to be who you could have been

Start step by step and you'll get there, and don't worry about failures

Start step by step and you'll get there,

and don't worry about failures

Start step by step and you'll get there,

and don't worry about failures

Start step by step and you'll get there,

and don't worry about failures

Start step by step and you'll get there,

and don't worry about failures

Start step by step and you'll get there,

and don't worry about failures

Start step by step and you'll get there,

and don't worry about failures

You are on the right path, keep working,
you are not defeated when you lose

You are on the right path, keep working,

you are not defeated when you lose

You are on the right path, keep working,

you are not defeated when you lose

You are on the right path, keep working,

you are not defeated when you lose

You are on the right path, keep working,

you are not defeated when you lose

You are on the right path, keep working,

you are not defeated when you lose

You are on the right path, keep working,

you are not defeated when you lose

Do not compare yourself to others, be
optimistic about the good things

Do not compare yourself to others, be
optimistic about the good things

Do not compare yourself to others, be
optimistic about the good things

Do not compare yourself to others, be
optimistic about the good things

Do not compare yourself to others, be
optimistic about the good things

Do not compare yourself to others, be
optimistic about the good things

Do not compare yourself to others, be
optimistic about the good things

Make criticism a reason for your progress, your attitude determines your direction

Make criticism a reason for your progress,
your attitude determines your direction
Make criticism a reason for your progress,
your attitude determines your direction
Make criticism a reason for your progress,
your attitude determines your direction
Make criticism a reason for your progress,
your attitude determines your direction
Make criticism a reason for your progress,
your attitude determines your direction
Make criticism a reason for your progress,
your attitude determines your direction

Made in the USA
Las Vegas, NV
26 December 2024

15352105R00066